Reflections of Harmony

REFLECTIONS OF HARMONY

Roxane Houston

SPRINGWOOD BOOKS

Garrick Street London

Printed in Great Britain by
Butler & Tanner Ltd, Frome and London
0 9059 4760 6

*Dedicated to all artists
in their perpetual struggle to achieve the
harmony of their own particular perfection.*

PREFACE

This book is autobiographical only in the sense that it applies to some of the many varied musical performances in which I have taken part, and is in no way intended to be a chronologically accurate account of my life's work so far. I have merely recorded some of the amusing, satisfying, exhilarating or disastrous episodes that go to make up the pattern of a singer's career.

CONTENTS

FIRST MOVEMENT

(affrettando con gioia)

I. ROYAL ACADEMY OF MUSIC

Full summer beat upon the wide front steps
Where I was standing, still and pensive,
Realising with regret that this would be
My final passing through those tall glass doors.
How many times had I swung carelessly or hurriedly
Or nervously through them and to the shaded hall
Into a different world, but one that suited me
So well that I felt more at home inside
Those walls than anywhere before.

For there I found my language spoken, all my
Thoughts, opinions, revelations
Understood, even approved, and certainly
Not smiled or gently mocked at, which had been
So often the result of venturing
To make my family and friends aware
Of what to me was normal and most necessary
For my well-being. No one before had ever
Fully understood the dedication or
Totality of my commitment, so I had been
A sort of rara avis for my family
To wonder at or to explain away.
Thus, overnight, I bade farewell to my
Unmourned and unregretted former life,
And built instead a new one for myself.

It did not seem like work, this manifold compulsion
Urging me to sample all the riches in that palace
Of harmonious endeavour – nor was I made
Aware that in that place it might be thought

Incongruous to cast oneself headlong into
Untiring industry and judge all else a waste of time.
There I met composers, pianists and singers;
There I sang their compositions, there
They played for my recitals and my lessons
And encouraged my endeavours in the field
Of orchestration. There we struggled to perfect
Our keyboard harmony, improve our listening ear,
And there, down in that stuffy, overcrowded
And inadequate canteen, we weighed the pros
And cons of all things musical in hot dispute,
And tossed opinions and ideas and contradictions
To and fro in vehement and happy argument.
There too, I made a friend of talent, drive and
Energy, who tragically was not to live
To see the fruits of his ideas and his unusual
Artistry fulfilled. But this was yet to come,
And in that final term there was no thought
Of anything but gaining a diploma
At the end of our endeavours.

(ii)

It had been warm that summer; endless
Weeks of weather wooing us away from work.
The lure of Regent's Park so near at hand
Had mostly emptied practice rooms and library,
And students sat or lay upon the scented grass,
Their books and manuscripts strewn round
In negligent disorder, while they fought
The sweet temptation to allow their thoughts to drift
Among the flowery retinue of summer
And the lazy drone of bees that sang
In descant to that tranquil lullaby.

It needed all our efforts to retreat
From that inviting borderland of sleep;
To keep our eyes upon our manuscript
And wrestle with the twine of counterpoint.
I can see him now, my first companion in
That battle for achievement in our chosen field,
His eyes locked hard upon that fragrant idyll
Yet unseeing of its beauty, so resolutely turned
Were they in fierce and inward concentration.
For minutes he would sit completely still,
His forehead furrowed, and his pencil ground
To splinters from the furious onslaught
Of his teeth. Then swiftly would his fingers
Grasp the mangled stump, and notes cascade
Across his manuscript at lightning speed,
So that they might be written down before
An interruption or his train of thought had failed.
Amused, admiring, envious, I would proceed
At hesitant and more pedestrian pace, often
Rueful of results that lacked the visionary
Spark that animated and invaded him.

(iii)

Now for the moment there was respite from
Routine and from the stress and tension of
Examinations. There remained but the
Adjustment to the life outside the shelter
Of this haven, to the knowledge that
All that we had learnt was to be put to test
Against the weight of our entire profession.
The prospect should have daunted and appalled
Us by its magnitude, but we possessed
That mixture of assurance and bravado,
Hope, determination and a faith in our ability
That not a word of wiser counsel would deflect

[13]

Throughout our future. What supreme and perfect
Confidence has Youth that takes no thought
To what *might* be, but knows what *must* be made
Of life!
    We shall not pass this way again,
At least, in our capacity as student. We had
Served our term of elementary learning and
Must place our talents, such as they might be,
At the disposal of the outer listening world,
And stand or fall by that far sterner judgement.

II. AUDITION

How strange to think the Wigmore Hall
Had ever struck such terror to my heart
As at that first audition! As I stood
With my accompanist, clutching my music
In my clammy hand I realised,
With sudden downward plunge of confidence,
The stiffness of the competition
Facing me. The artists' room was full
Of singers, mainly tall and statuesque,
Flamboyant in their colours and their style,
Their voices clear and resonant that carried
With the minimum of effort. Worst of all,
Most of them appeared to know each other,
And displayed an easy camaraderie,
Carelessly excluding me, unnoticed in my corner.
Oh, how I envied them that calm assurance
I had been so certain I possessed,
But which now seemed to have deserted me!

I heard the first name called and saw
A tall man turn his head and smile,
Detach himself from several friends
And disappear into the hall.
The artists' room was silent now,
And we could hear the Handel aria
Sung in a resonant full baritone
Of powerful ease and accuracy.
He followed it with 'Vision fugitive'
From Massanet's 'Hérodiade'.
Both line and phrasing were impeccable,
And at the end one half expected

An ovation, but of course none came; instead,
A muffled conversation in the hall
Took place before the baritone returned,
As cool and imperturbable as ever.
After that each summons followed thick and fast,
And as I listened so my spirits sank.
Anxiety akin to panic flooded
Through my very bones, and for the first time
In my life I knew the agony of stage-fright –
That terror and despondency that creeps
Up from the feet to make the heart begin
To pound, the mouth go dry, and round the throat
The self-inflicted stranglehold of failure
Tighten its inexorable grip.
For who was I to put my fresh-trained voice
Against such massive giants as these? For here
Were lyric tenors, sonorous deep basses,
Steely bright sopranos, both dramatic
And full lyric, and a coloratura mezzo
Who sang the florid aria from Rossini's
'Cenerentola' with a technique and control
That held her listening colleagues spellbound
With appreciation and approval. She took
The complicated runs and roulades at
A speed that would have terrified most vocal
Cinderellas, and the ice-clear sparkling
Fioriture of her ending almost drew
Spontaneous applause. But I was numb
And could not move a muscle. If I were called
To follow that performance – ! But the Gods
That day were kind. A small but sweet-toned tenor
Brought us back to earth and let us hear
That he at least was mortal. I regained
My equilibrium, for now at last
A coldly calm determination banished
All my nerves, and when my name was called

I left the artists' room quite steadily,
And found myself with my accompanist
Upon the platform, even smiling at my auditors –
Two men of fame and stature, both well known
In the profession, who then asked me
What I wished to sing. It was Zerlina's
Aria from Act One of 'Don Giovanni'
Where she begs forgiveness from Masetto,
Her betrothed ... but here the action
Of the piece almost eluded me,
So great was my astonishment, relief and wonder
At the hall's acoustics, true but mellowed,
Yet revealing all the voice, and certainly
Removing any need to force the tone
As in so many concert halls.
This quaint Victorian emporium
With its pastoral decor, red carpeting,
Plush seats and heavy polished doors,
Gave back with evident affection
A flattering facsimile of sound,
As if in thanks to those unnumbered artists
Who for years had blessed its peaceful walls
With what was best of all they had to give.
My spirits rose still further, for the hall
Was bright with sunshine streaming through
The skylight in the centre of the roof.
By the time I sang the Cavatina
From 'The Pearl Fishers', I felt relaxed
And confident, so much at home
I knew I did full justice to myself –
And Bizet too, I hope.

Then I was back inside the artists' room,
No longer an intruder in
An unfamiliar milieu, but
A proven member of my great profession.

I shall not be so much afraid another time.
Auditions are a test of nerve,
Of one's capacity to give the best
Immediately, to light up like a lamp
Responding to a switch; no time
To warm up mentally or vocally.
In that respect I had not failed,
And even if my voice were not the type
They sought at this audition for their opera,
I was now supplied with solid proof
Of my ability to keep control
Upon my nervous system, make it work
For and not against me, not
As negative an asset as it sounds,
For there are times when nerves and over-
Consciousness of self obtrude upon
Performances, reducing their effect
To mere routine. Impossible to feel
That inner sparkle every time, but
Fortunate the artist who, no matter
What his physical or mental state,
Can conjure up an instant rapport with
His audience, persuading them to feel
That each performance is his best and he
Perpetually illumined from within.

III. 'PALM COURT'

I should have known, of course.
I should have known, or guessed!
But I was green
And gullible, and keen –
And also for the moment
Broke.
So I believed this agent from the theatre –
He who said he'd make of me a star –
When he told me fame was waiting
Round the corner – well, not far
Actually, somewhere called Scunthorpe
In the north-eastern region ... Nothing.
Not a solitary bell,
Rang out to give this innocent
Young lamb a warning knell –
Not even when he told me this
'Palm Court' engagement was
To sing each evening at the Bell
Hotel (where all the local
Gentry held their annual
Hunt Ball!)
Well, fifteen pounds was fifteen pounds.
Riches! So I quelled
Whatever streak of sanity prevailed,
And left the comfort of the world I knew
For pastures that seemed greener.

Mind you, after I'd arrived,
The cosy 'Palm Court' image
Faded just a little, though the hotel lounge

Was vast and certainly had palms –
Though not for me. Instead,
Still uncomplaining, I was led
Through endless winding corridors
Within its nether regions – (Very odd!
Perhaps someone mistook me for a chambermaid!)
And passing through a solid oak wood door,
We entered what I was assured
Was certainly the centre of
All local culture, quite undoubtedly the hub
Of Scunthorpe's scintillating universe,
(Though unmistakably
A pub!)

Perhaps it would be wise
To gloss over my reactions then –
(Self-denigration is so wearing,
Far too salutary!)
Suffice to say I grit my teeth,
Did all the usual British things
(Except the bit about
The upper lip – one cannot sing
In that condition) – but I swore
Black vengeance on that agent's soul.

After a while my fury cooled
And I began
To see the funny side of it.
How many singers, after all,
Having reached the pinnacle
Of their success in later years,
Could boast of having sung
In something called a 'four-ale bar'?
(This being, mark you, an insignia
Of elegance – the upper stratum
Of the drinking world!)

[20]

If the customers had asked
For singing, they should have it
In abundance!
Three groups of three
Between the comic turns,
They said to me,
Was usual – that made fifty four
In all during that week –
Almost every song
I knew, and some I didn't
But could read from the pianist's
Old and desecrated score.
I had already, somewhat scornfully,
(For such a minute auditorium!)
Refused the proffered microphone,
Which they assured me I would need
If I wished to be heard
At all: and in the panic of the first
Few songs I felt they could be right.
My rough and cheerful audience,
Fully charged with alcohol and bonhomie,
Chattered blithely on at first, but gradually
Their laughter and the sound of clinking glass
Grew less, and they began to listen.
Confidence returned, and with it came
That heady aura of success so sweet
To any artist when he holds
An audience in his hand.
I felt myself assume ascendancy
Over them all, even forgot
For minutes at a time,
My uncongenial surroundings.

Folk-song, ballad, aria –
During that week I gave them
Everything that needed airing

From my repertoire: the accompanist
Surprisingly played like an angel;
Even Butterfly's 'One fine day'
Did not defeat him.
In between the bouts of song
The comic turn took over –
A girl and a man both dressed
As gypsies, whose noisy opening number
With accordion, full blast into
The microphone, assailed my ears
And senses till the scene
Became unreal and unbelievable.
The jokes were mainly old
And richly blue, but by that time
It seemed that nothing mattered
And I weakly laughed with all the rest,
Who soon gave way to mirthful paroxysms,
Unrestrained and inexplicable.

Later on the stuffy atmosphere grew thick
With every kind of acrid smoke:
But these delighted customers
Were kind, insisting I should try
Their local beverage to soothe my throat.
I drank a mouthful, found it quite enough,
And watched in sick dismay as
Pint after thick and oily pint
Of somebody's Milk Stout accumulated
On my table by the stage.
Fearful to offend, in desperation I looked round
For help. My frantic eye made contact
With a frail and trembling sage
Who sat nearby and beat time with his foot.
He understood my meaning in a flash,
And under cover of each burst of fresh
Applause, shot out a skinny, shaking hand,

Removed a pint, and with a bright
And toothless grin in my direction,
Swallowed down that nauseous brew.
Fascinated, I lost count of
The number he consumed without
Much visible effect.
My admiration for the ancient grew
As that appalling week progressed:
He became my only friend,
And must have missed me
When I left, for surely
Never in his meagre life
Had he been given so much
Richly protein bounty!

All at once, by some divine compassion,
It was Saturday. The pub was full,
A compliment, my fellow artists said,
To all of us. Our fame had spread,
The management was pleased and would be sure
To ask us back again.
(Oh no! Dear God forbid!)
But oddly enough, when it was over
And I had listened to some quaint farewells –
('Good-bye then, lass, you're much
Too good for this old dump!'
Imagine! What a reference
For future use! My flatmates, too,
Were suitably convulsed) – I thought of it
Another way, almost with affection.
Who was I, after all,
To cavil at a job of work,
But a month-or-two old graduate
Of a musical academy,
Full of fat opinion of her worth?
These people were my audience,

Not entirely what I'd hoped for,
I admit, but still, they'd listened
With remarkable attention,
And applauded at the end and not the middle –
They might, of course, have talked the whole way through!

So after all it had not been too bad
Or too degrading an experience:
And when next day at home
The telephone began to ring,
Inviting me to go and sing
'Elijah' somewhere – I forget –
I even forgave the agent who
So grossly had misled me, for
Once more the sun was out.

IV. CALLAS AT COVENT GARDEN

(i)

On scintillating gala nights the audience
Outshone in some respects the blazoned stage,
For there the gems were mere facsimile,
But those in stalls and balcony were real;
And even after all the lights were dimmed
Throughout that vast and jewel-pointed darkness,
Cufflink and tiara winked, pearl tiepins
Glinted with reflected light – all London's
Cultural élite, sweet-perfumed and
Pomaded, had turned out to do full justice
To a glittering occasion. For
When London feels that she is honoured,
Few citizens know how better to return
The compliment with old world courtesy
And style, to dazzle even in the glare
Of Coronation summer. There is in the air
The residue of sweet Havana previously
Enjoyed with Scotch or dry Martini, or
With light aperitifs to suit
This bright and festive evening in
The elegant Crush Bar.
Though few in that smart audience may know
The intricacies of that famous score,
All will respond with energy and fervour
To the galvanising name of Callas
As Aida, and an Amneris –
Perhaps not so well known to London ears,
But matching her in voice if not in stature –
Giulietta Simionato, small,
Compact, but with a vocal instrument

[25]

Of fire and steel, controlled, magnificent,
A worthy mistress of her famous slave.

(ii)

And on to this vast operatic canvas
Timidly among the giants I crept,
A few short months out of the sheltered shell
Of my academy, with twenty-three
Mixed voices, to enlarge the aural spectrum
And to fill each empty corner of
That multi-coloured acreage of stage –
In short, an operatic extra with
Egyptian wig that would have done full credit
To a Hollywood production of
'Antony and Cleopatra' – long
Black curls and hanging fringe that fell across
My eyes, (always a tiresome problem of
Some magnitude in my career, because
My visual range is two yards at the most
In any detail, and has led to some
Disasters and distractions on the stage,
When contact lenses went astray, or make-up
Or false hair became incarcerated
In my eye just at the moment when
I had to join the singing throng
Upon gigantic staircase or a high
And dangerous extension to a stage.)
This wretched disability I later learned
I shared with Madame Callas, who would feel her way
Across the stage with grace and cunning,
Even at a moment of high drama
And full vocal power. It took some courage
To ignore the lurking dangers of poor sight,
Relegating it to some deep watchful
Corner of the mind, and so to concentrate

Upon the music and its spiritual demands.
But this she did, while circumnavigating
Scenery and soloists and over
Sixty members of the chorus and
The supernumeraries who helped to dress
The stage with splendour. Fifteen stone she may
Have been, but I was never to forget
The dusky cream and cognac quality
Of voice that spread its richly warm and tender
Brilliance upon her spellbound audience,
Enveloping us in a balm of radiance
That subtly soothed the spirit and the senses
To a willing and complete surrender.

(iii)

In retrospect I doubt the wisdom
Of selecting extra chorus
To enlarge the scene without enough
Rehearsal on the stage, at least
To let us know what to expect:
For everywhere I stood, it seemed
That I was masking someone's vision
Of conductor, or was in the way
Of some exalted soloist's approach;
Then unseen hands would push or pull me
From their path until I felt
That I had wandered by mistake
Into some thunderous arena
Of an ancient time and place
In which I had no part.
If you would multiply my own
Bewilderment by twenty-three,
You could imagine the confusion
That ensued beneath the great
And ringing choruses we sang.

Welsh and English voices – and
Australian – besought us in their
Various vernacular –
(Rich and wry, but to the point!)
To move ourselves far from their sight,
Go home where we belonged and *never*
Try usurping their positions
On that stage again! Eventually,
My sense of humour, never at
The best of times entirely under
Strict control, evinced itself
In silent laughter that upset
My vocal line and thus infected
My immediate companions.
Perhaps it was the black and woolly wigs
Incongruously crowning Welsh and English
And Australian faces, northern eyes
Light against the darkened skins,
And muttered sentences concerned with
Football scores and daily trivia,
Whenever conversation from the crowd
Was needed. Had there been a microphone – !
That, at least, was never needed
For the voices were projected
With untrammelled freedom, riding
Effortlessly high above
The huge orchestral forces
From the pit. The overwhelming,
Sheer magnificence of sound
Left me transfixed, immovable,
And sent a tense and tingling
Sensation down my spine.
Unnoticed, from the wings, I watched
Amneris' great scene, saw how
She took command both with her voice
And acting of the role – so small

And slight in stature, but attracting
All attention from the moment
She stepped out on to the stage.
When she had ended and the wild applause
Had died, another vocal treat
Was yet to come – the final scene
When Callas came once more into her own,
Tearing to the heart of this
Stark, tragic situation, voice and
Presence unforgettable.

(iv)

Fascinating to compare
These vocal high priestesses –
One at the peak of her achievement,
The other still a rising star
Upon the musical firmament –
But both possessors of that strange,
Dynamic quality that generates
Excitement, grips an audience by the throat
And brings it cheering to its feet.
Such artists, by the stern totality
Of their commitment, carry with them
An encircling charisma that attracts,
Involves and conquers irresistibly,
And London and the operatic world
Accorded them the final accolade,
Rising upon the tide of their success
In royal response and high acclaim
To lay bright garlands at their feet.

V. A TALE OF HOFFMANN

'Concert version – "Tales of Hoffmann"?
Of course,' I said without ado,
In answer to the telephoned enquiry,
Thinking of those top E flats,
Those sparkling top Ds and Cs
So seldom needed, but kept fresh
For rare engagements such as these.
Not oratorio this time,
As it had often been of late,
Which I enjoyed, but hardly used
The higher echelons of voice.
I assumed that I was meant
To sing the doll, Olympia,
A role that I had never played
In full, though many times had sung
Her famous automated song.
'It's all *three* roles,' the voice went on
Apologetically, 'and by the way,
We're doing "Faust" – the concert version
Also – for the second half,
So would you kindly sing the role
Of Marguerite as well?'

The music club was quite well known,
The fee was high, and I was free
That evening, so there seemed no valid
Reason to refuse, though four
Such roles was quite substantial fare
That would require Olympic stamina.
My singing teacher blenched a little
When he heard the huge amount

Margaret Moncrieff and the Author

I wished to sing.
'Coloratura, lyric and
Dramatic! Well!' he exclaimed,
Regarding me
A little enigmatically:
'It will be interesting to see
If one high lyric voice contains
Sufficient versatility
. For all of these . . .
However, let's get down to work.'

Fortunately, we had time
Upon our side, and since I was
A virtual débutante upon
The full professional scene,
I had far fewer interruptions
Than I would have suffered, had I been
A busy artist travelling
The country up and down,
Continually in demand
And having new works thrust upon
A well-trained and receptive mind.

I studied for hours every day.
It seemed to me I had no friends,
No one to talk to, (though I shared
A flat with two long-suffering
Companions, saner far than I,
Who worked the normal hours each day
And spent their evenings in the glow
Of warm conviviality.)
My mind was taken up with dolls
And courtesans, consumptive girls
(Who must no longer sing for fear
Of death!) and later on, with Faust
And Marguerite, until my head
Began to swim and notes to dance

Before my eyes. But gradually
The characters began to fit
Their music and became
Real flesh and blood: I understood
Their sentiments and problems and
Could sympathise with poor Antonia's
Desire to use her voice once more
For her dead mother's sake....
My teacher entered into this
Great operatic venture with
A zeal and energy surpassing
Mine. (He told me afterwards
That he had been aghast at all
That I had taken on,
But had not wished to blunt
Such fierce determination!)
So I continued, blithely
Unaware of his concern, and as
The busy weeks went by we found
That through my disciplined routine,
Not only did each role become
More natural to my voice, but I
Had even gained in vocal strength.
The programme then was possible;
I could sustain the interest
And disregard its length.

Now there can come a certain time,
As every working artist knows,
When one has studied for too long,
Too fiercely concentrated and
Too vocally obsessed,
When interest begins to fade,
And soon the music too can pall,
Become far too familiar, stale,
Fit only to be cast aside.

[33]

I had almost reached this sated
Danger point when fortunately it
Was time to put my efforts to the test.

Just one rehearsal on the day;
No time for hidden subtleties
Or working out the vocal balance
Or the full ensemble niceties:
As long as pitch and time were true,
The choral entries accurate,
The high notes loud and ringing
And the climaxes exciting –
And if each voice was supercharged
With suitable emotion, then
Who cared about rubato
Or less time to breathe than usual
In the fury of allegro?

He was a most efficient man,
This popular conductor, who
Had spent almost fifteen years
In charge of this particular
Society. All sorts of artists
Knew him and admired his work,
For he was pliant with his singers,
Firm towards his chorus and
Accommodating to the whims
And difficulties of the brass
Or woodwind when the temperature
Affected pitch, and was alert
When instrumentalists became
Enmeshed within the labyrinth
Of fast conflicting rhythms
That might well have led to chaos
In the ranks. For he was *safe*,
And later on that evening steered us

Nimbly through both works with ease
And confidence and ardour,
And the minimum of fuss.

We soon became accustomed to
The evening's strenuous demands,
Developed what all athletes know
As 'second-wind', and settled down
To electrify our audience to
A mounting pitch of wild, pent-up
Enthusiasm that soon found
Expression in the constant burst
Of loud spontaneous applause
That followed every aria.
As we warmed up, so did the packed
And curtained hall, and soon we all
Became aware of our discomfort.
Dr Miracle's stiff shirt
Had wilted in the heat –
(He looked less sinister like that!)
And beads of perspiration lay
Upon his brow; while Hoffmann's
Countenance became suffused
With rich and unaccustomed colour,
Hardly matching his distraught
And agonised reaction to
The final horrifying pallor
Of his dead Antonia's cheek.
(In this case her consumptive flush
Remained long after her last note
And well into the interval –
When we were able to refresh
Ourselves in cooler air!)

And so to 'Faust', and to the different
Character of Marguerite.

[35]

I found it restful to remain
The same soprano voice throughout
The second half, not have to change
Technique from that of living doll
To darker and maturer tones
For the voluptuous courtesan
Giulietta, finally to find
The floating lyric line required
For wan Antonia; and at the end
To feel, amid the long ovation,
A hitherto unknown elation,
Basking, as did all my colleagues, in
That heady sense of exultation,
Tinged with exhaustion and relief,
That comes to every artist in
Achievement's vivid satisfaction
When the evening's work is over
And the curtain has come down.

VI. AT THE MERCURY

(i)

It seemed to me impossible that anyone could dance
Upon that minute stage. The curtains hung in heavy folds
That overlapped upon much needed space behind the scenes,
And sometimes made it difficult for an effective exit
Or an entry that involved strict timing or precision.
These dancers of the Ballet Rambert knew exactly how much
Room they were allowed for pirouette or jump or turn,
Or point of toe or stretch of arm; not only must they learn
The dance itself – they must accept the added discipline
Of circumnavigating limitations of their space,
Built cleverly into the basic choreography.
It says a great deal for their physical control that
Never once did anyone collide or even narrowly
Avoid disaster, though sometimes musicians in the 'pit' –
Floor space between the front row of the auditorium
And the stage itself – had now and then to duck their heads
As someone danced too far downstage, and pointed foot
Swept past to miss an eye, it seemed, by inches.

The Musical Director was my friend of student days,
Whose drive and energy had helped considerably
To draw me into circles where my versatility
In music would be useful – so he said! I found myself
Time after time invited to portray a character
In some new composition he had written, or to try
Some vocal part whose tessitura lay in doubtful area –
In fact, a guinea pig for musical experiment,
And this I found was excellent experience
For many of the modern works I was to learn
Much later on. His latest composition at that time

Was for the ballet 'Les Chimères', depicting strange,
Fantastic creatures half of human origin, and half
Of some weird prehistoric bird. For one of these he wrote
A high soprano part of graceful, floating melody,
That often lay exclusively above the stave,
Stretching the voice to full capacity. I loved to sing
Those sweeping phrases, weaving in and out across the threads
Of his accompaniment of clarinet and harp and cello,
Blending in a patterned filigree as delicate
As lace: and interspun about it like a spider's web,
The gossamer glissando of the harp would rise and fall
In rippling arc like mist of spray tossed by a wayward wind.

None of this was easy, even with a music stand
That stayed in place, or with a light of adequate degree,
Or even with the sight of the director's hand
So that we might preserve the rhythm and precision
Of the piece. Instead, it was decided that the voice
Should be a disembodied adjunct to the instruments,
And float mysteriously across the stage from some
Unseen position. Thus I stood among the dusty curtains
In a darkened corner well behind the scenes, and took
With me a torch in case the light upon the music stand
Was shattered by a dancer's flying leap. I had to hold
My copy in a stringent grasp, for all the time I sang
The curtains swayed and trembled at the lightest touch
And threatened to engulf me. Even this was not the worst
Of all the difficulties which we had to face. Since dancing
Was the prime consideration, it was thus essential
For the dancers' sake that we did not indulge in undue
Variations of their speed. For me, this meant no licence
Was permitted when I faced an awkward octave leap,
Or hazardous approach to some high-arching phrase that lay
In perilous proximity to notes beyond my range:
Yet if a dancer needed extra seconds to complete
A movement that involved a leap of greater height

Than usual, we would have no choice but to accommodate
Him with a slackening of pace. This in itself did not
Present a problem to the players, nor indeed to me,
Had I been able from my hidden vantage point to see
The guiding movement from the pit. But as it was,
I could see nothing but the pool of light upon my score,
And now and then a glimpse of dancers passing through my
    line
Of vision, so was forced to take my time from them.
Somehow these difficulties were resolved, and we would find
A level of performance that would finally reveal
The beauty and enchantment of that deep and inner vision
Conceived by the composer, to be translated later,
Through the artistry of choreographer and dancers,
Into the finished tapestry of this intriguing and
Most subtle art, this living poetry of form and movement
From which all evidence of effort has been expurgated,
And only ease of grace in its simplicity remains.

(ii)

We did not always work beneath such difficult conditions.
There were times when I would be required to sing before
The curtains – once for a modern ballet which was danced to
    music
By Sibelius – four songs not often sung,
But eminently suited to its atmosphere and mood.
The Rambert had a reputation for experiment
In style, for exploration into methods of expression
Far beyond the narrow confines of the classical
Tradition, and in this new ballet all these fresh ideas
Were melded in an abstract form, where ambiguity
And symbolism had replaced the more direct approach
Towards the audience. It was in the second song
That I became uneasily aware of someone staring
Fixedly at me, a man whose hair and general style

[39]

Of dress proclaimed a background very different from
His neighbours, more mature, more positive, yet at this
   moment
Totally at sea. He looked as if he had arrived
By unremembered means upon some unknown island, and
No longer knew the season of the year nor time of day.
Now and then he cast a tentative, bewildered glance
Towards the dancers and from them to me. Perhaps
He felt, by studying my words, that he could forcibly
Extract the hidden meaning of the choreography.
I could have told him that the songs themselves had no
   connection
With the ballet, but were used entirely to create
A solid background for inconsequential thoughts
And images, elusive and intangible, a wisp
Of primitive significance as clouded and obscure
As writing carved on ancient stone. If only he had been
Content to let the waves of sound and movement overtake
His consciousness, to be submerged and resurrected by
The alternating moods without the need to have the details
Spelt out for his inspection, he might even then have gleaned
Some understanding. But he was too practical
A man, and at the end of it he raised his head,
And as I bowed towards the audience, gave me a look
Of such reproach and latent indignation that I felt
I should have tendered an apology! How sad to think
How much in life must have been missed by people like
   himself,
Unable to appreciate all that is unexpressed
And delicate in art – the faint suggestion, not defined
Too sharply in its boundaries of light and shade,
Whose accent and emotion is not forcefully displayed,
Yet effortlessly reaches out to touch the heart and mind.

VII. CELEBRITY CONCERT

(i)

Hundreds of faces staring at me,
Hundreds of voices joining in
The opening hymn; the Chapel full,
Ground floor to balcony a sea
Of sound and breathing, and the air
Vibrating to the ancient tongue.
And I, who know no Welsh, stand still
In silence to receive this blessing
And this rousing challenge – alien
To them save by the linking tie
Of melody. And as they sing,
That challenge, wordlessly conveyed,
Is unmistakable and clear:
'You are in Wales, the land of song!
So since you've come, let's hear
The best a Londoner can do!'

At first I felt unnerved by this,
Was tempted there and then to use
More voice than necessary to
Impress these natural vocalists:
Even if I should abuse
My vocal cords, I thought, at least
They will have heard the full extent
Of my ability!
Since then, of course, unnumbered times
Have I returned to Wales to sing,
Become accustomed to this trait,
And so no longer feel I bring
Unwanted coals to Newcastle.

It still seems strange to stand within
The centre of a pulpit when
Depicting Violetta, or a
Marguerite or Mimi in
Emotional duet beside
A full-voiced baritone
Or tenor, singing without a hint
Of English church embarrassment,
Or that inhibiting restraint
That strangles voices in the throat
And drowns a song at infancy.
Often were these singers Welsh
Themselves and laughed to scorn
My hesitation. So at last
I found that I must disregard
My strange surroundings, try to feel
That we were standing on a stage,
And with an orchestra instead
Of the piano or the organ
That would often be the sole
Accompaniment; and only then
Would I be able to enact
The eloquence of tragedy
Or thwarted love, or any of the
Operatic situations
Calling for the maximum
Dramatic histrionic.

Singing to the Welsh is like
A feast in which all join, for they
Are quite unable to remain
Impassive listeners. They feel
The weight of sorrow or the lift
Of great elation, and are swift
To recognise and understand
A nuance or a hint of hidden

Comedy, and so persuade
The best performance from the artist.
To have your audience involved
In what you do is half the battle,
And in everyone in Wales
There lurks an operatic singer,
Who but for altered circumstance
Might well have sung in this same place –
A graduate to Covent Garden
And the international field.

After enthusiastic thanks
And plaudits from the Mayor and other
Local hierarchy, I felt
Relieved that London had not lost
Its singing reputation yet.
So to the local station and
The late night train to London via
Cardiff; early on the morrow
A rehearsal and recording –
Somehow to be at one's best
Throughout the day until the end
Of this exhausting run of work.

(ii)

Now it is far too dark to see
The valleys and the hills of Wales
That had enchanted me that morning
From the train – that varied green
Of undulating land enriched
With foliage faintly tinged with red,
As soft September overtook
The fading summer. Here I sit
In restful silence, leaning back
Against my seat, my eyes half-closed,

And let the evening's images recede.
All had gone well, and I had been
Most cordially invited back; so
For the moment here was peace
And opportunity to charge
My batteries anew before
The coming session. Every artist
Has an urgent need of these
Few quiet moments of repose
To let the tension dissipate,
Replenish his resources and
Find time to re-assimilate
The healing stillness of the spirit.
Seldom had I been so glad
Of being silent and alone....
But soon my reverie is shattered
By the braking of the train
Approaching Cardiff, and the guard
Arrives to tell me he will lock
My door in case the football crowd
About to come on board should make
A nuisance of themselves, disturb
My sleep. For he, of course, has seen
My concert make-up (which I had
No time to deal with in my haste
To reach the station), and the flowers
That had been given me; has guessed
My evening's occupation, and
Assigns himself my guardian for
The coming journey. At first I felt
That his solicitude might be
Excessive, but I soon found out
The wisdom of his strange decision.

So we sidled into Cardiff,
Station platform echoing

[44]

To prehistoric shouts and cries
In some wild, primitive vernacular;
And multi-coloured, woollen-muffled
Merry monsters surging through
The narrow doors, their feet askew,
Unsteadily, beyond control,
Good-humoured but awash with beer
And bonhomie and laughter and
Affection for each other, full
Of bright anticipation of
The morrow's contest versus England.

Through every sleeping county fled
The loaded train, a snaking shaft
Of moving light awaking shadows
By the track, a multiplicity
Of voices roaring out of tune,
That rose and fell and rose again
To leave their echoes hovering
Upon the shattered air ... but I
Was listening to other sounds,
My ears and mind retentive still
To music of more sensitive appeal,
Whose gentle residue was mingled
With the flying landscape,
Unidentifiable
Except occasionally when spire
Or turret of a village church
Reached up to pierce a skyline that
Was barely now perceptible,
Reiteration of a faith
Proclaimed to us the passing pilgrims.

At last the singing from the train
Grew less and faded to a gradual
Halt – lulled by the dull

Insistent rhythm of the fleeting wheels.
Something approaching silence
Fell upon the tired night, and soon
My beneficent custodian
Came round to visit me once more,
With unexpected and most welcome
Cup of tea, to reassure
His prisoner that all was well.
I thanked him gratefully and took
From my bouquet a crimson rose
To fasten to his buttonhole.
Smiling, he sniffed its scent and said,
With slight derisive jerk of head
Towards the shadowed corridor:
'They're welcome to their football, but
Give me the opera instead!'

SECOND MOVEMENT

(allegro con spirito)

I. GLYNDEBOURNE

Only one short hour away, and yet we crossed
A line into a different dimension.
One short hour away, and we were driving through
The narrow winding lanes of Sussex in
The April early morning haze, past hedgerows
Fresh with hint of April greenery,
And April air a messenger to fill
Our winter-weary lungs with delicate foretaste
Of Summer's close proximity. How strange
That all this should result from that December day's
Audition in a dingy London studio,
Whose rain-bespattered windows masked the light
Of Winter's dreary afternoon – when only three
Of us from out of all that eager crowd
Of young sopranos there were chosen, fortunate
And blessed spirits for this new Elysium.

Our charabanc swept down a curving hill,
And all at once we left behind the high-banked hedge
That previously had blocked our view, and saw
What lay below. Although expected, all drew in
A sudden breath, for this was far beyond
Our most extravagant imagining.
A broad and winding drive led past the sweep of lawn
Towards the tall, serenely gracious mansion,
Perfect in proportion and in symmetry,
Flanked by graceful sentinels of beech and
Yew and cedar, to protect it from encroachment
From the noisy outer world. It was
A vision stamped indelibly upon the mind,

And after all the years that followed this,
My first incredulous impression, I can still,
Without a conscious effort of my will –
In fact, it comes unbidden now and then –
Conjure up this setting as I saw it first,
And hear the crunch of wheels upon the drive,
And at the same time find that I can even smell
The scented air of that fresh April day.

The history of Glyndebourne's unobtrusive start,
Of the theatre built as wedding present for
John Christie's bride, a Mozart singer of distinction,
Was to all of us, of course, familiar;
But when we saw its actual presence in the grounds
I remember thinking it at first
An unreal sight, incredible, incongruous
Within its most exquisite setting. Banks of flowers
Of every colour and description, smoothly green
Well-tended lawns, a high-walled garden leading to
A tennis court; a croquet lawn encircled by
A tall dark hedge; a shaded sunken dell
Enclosed by shrubs and leaning trees, and further on,
More trees of ancient lineage that cast
Enormous shadows on the mirrored lake
On which were floating small green-crested ducks –
An English rural scene, this pastel watercolour,
Even to the cows upon the nearby hill
That welcomed us with liquid and incurious gaze.
This dreaming stillness was, of course, deceptive,
For it hid the strenuous energy
And animation lavished on the operas
In preparation, detailed and meticulous
And totally absorbing....

Our charabanc passed on beneath a graceful arch
Into a quiet courtyard, where it stopped
Beside the entrance to a covered way. Here
We disembarked, and from then on all semblance to a
Peaceful country life abruptly ceased
As we were all precipitated into new
And stricter patterns of existence.
Time became irrelevant and meaningless
Except where it denoted the beginning
Of the operatic season, and the end of our
Intense preoccupation with rehearsal
Leading to the highest peak of a perfection
Here regarded as the norm, instead of
Something strange and wonderful beyond the usual
Limits of performance. For although
The discipline was stern and close attention paid
To every minute detail, there was still
Another welcome adjunct to a good production,
That of extra time for preparation,
The added luxury of lack of haste:
Time for thorough study of the music and
For the development of character
Within the various roles, so that the artists gained
An insight and assurance that revealed itself
Most clearly in the quality of their performance.

Well did Glyndebourne earn its famous reputation!
For how, with such a team as worked therein,
Could anything have failed or not attained its highest
Standard? For me an endless fascination
Lay within the period before the stage
Production would begin, the moment when,
After the independent study of the roles,
The chorus work and separate orchestral sessions,

We all of us together had to spend
Some further hours of musical rehearsal
To achieve a perfect balance, and to blend
The varied forces into one artistic whole.
Responsibility for this lay with
The eminent Fritz Busch, under whose command
And expert guidance all the elegance
And wit and gaiety of 'Figaro',
'Idomeneo's' stylised beauty,
And 'Don Giovanni's' great dramatic strength,
Were brought to full fruition with the ease
And accuracy of our long acquaintance
With the scores. This work took place
In one of the two big restaurants – that is,
It would become a restaurant at night
During the season, but was now rehearsal room
Of adequate dimension to accommodate
The Royal Philharmonic Orchestra as well as
Soloists and chorus, and the ancient oak
That grew out from the floor and through the roof,
Staking its prior claim to that small plot of land
And jealous of its access to the open sky.
(One very soon learned not to feel surprise
At the endearing whimsicalities of
Glyndebourne's owner and inspired initiator.)
His quizzical and puckish sense of humour,
Allied to his charm and kind benevolence,
Penetrated every corner of this most
Unusual place, and everyone who worked
Beneath his friendly aegis, felt a welcome sense
Of being honoured guests. Christian names
Were used down to the youngest stage assistant,
And the first night bottle of champagne
Presented to the soloists, must have astounded
Many of the foreign artists, unaccustomed
To this added gentle courtesy.

[52]

I can never visualise that sturdy tree
Round which the large rehearsal room was built,
Without the figure of the Maestro on his stool,
Leaning back against its gnarled support,
His pale blue eyes half blind with inner concentration
As he listened with acute and critical intent
To ravishing duets and arias,
To trios and ensembles and sextets,
Nurturing them to their full maturity
With love and care of long experience.
For me, at this first hearing of their finished state,
Their beauty and invention set a seal
Upon perfection such as we were never
To forget, and hours passed by as minutes
In the warming glow of Mozart's genius.
(How desolate the world must be for those
Who have not ears to notice him!)

(iii)

Then we were on the stage, where music merged
And melted into movement of a pattern
Set for us by the producer, Carl Ebert,
One time famous actor from Berlin,
Known to all of us as 'The Professor',
Brilliant instigator of so many
Unexpected innovations and effects,
Total in authority, yet able to
Cajole, persuade and charm his multi-national singers
To complete capitulation to his will.
No simple matter this, for some of them,
Particularly the Italians, spoke no English.
However, to Professor Ebert this presented
Little difficulty, for he often spoke
In several fluent.languages within
The space of a single sentence, turning back

[53]

To English for the benefit of chorus
And the listening stage staff. In general
He was smiling and urbane, but once we saw
And felt the rare expression of his anger.
It happened in Act II of 'Figaro' –
Only the second rehearsal on the stage –
In the boudoir of the Countess Almaviva,
During Susanna's solo with the difficult
Stage business of attiring Cherubino
In a woman's dress and cap, and teaching him
To walk more gracefully. Already twice
This had not been successful, and we saw
That the Professor grew displeased. And then,
During the third attempt, the dress became
Entangled hopelessly around the page's legs,
Susanna's voice tailed off, and all three singers on
The littered stage dissolved in helpless laughter.

Not so Professor Ebert! This was *not*
What he had been accustomed to and now,
Reverting in his fury to his native tongue,
He poured upon the poor unfortunate
American Susanna and the hapless
Cherubino all his pent-up wrath
With all the force and ringing resonance
Of his great actor's voice, the fearsome
Diatribe occasionally punctuated
By his stamping feet, while with his hands
He clutched and tore at his superb white hair.

Not a single person moved, the singers,
(Only one of whom, the Countess, understood
All he was saying), standing riveted with shock
Upon the stage, their laughter frozen on their lips.
We of the chorus, silent in our seats down in
The auditorium, thanked God that this tirade

Was not directed at our heads, but wishing
All the same that we might understand
More of his actual words, although the gist
Of what he said was all too menacingly clear.
(Oh, what a splendid language to be angry in
With all those guttural and close-packed consonants!
Somehow it was a privilege to hear them strike
White-hot upon the air, excoriating in effect) –
But now stage manager and other members
Of his team moved swiftly in upon the scene
To separate the seething combatants,
Apprehensive that the famous 'singers'
Temperament' might well be roused in fierce
Retaliation for such treatment, and the stage
Dissolve in some unseemingly fracas.

Soothing voices calmed both shattered nerves
And egos momentarily crushed, and someone murmured
'Tea? – Perhaps an early break?' – the English
Panacea for dramas of whatever
Nationality; and soon the volatile
Professor let himself be coaxed towards refreshment
And repose, while the rearguard remnants
Of the battlefield retreated to repair
Their ruffled dignity and so regain
Their equilibrium ... and in the quiet theatre –
Sole residue of that gargantuan gust of anger –
Several tinsel tufts of snow-white hair,
Pale and wilted lilies of the field,
Floated on the surface of the empty stage.

(iv)

A fortnight after this there came a day
When troubles such as these were left behind,
And we had settled down into a new routine:

[55]

Three operas already in performance,
With several weeks to go before rehearsals
For the final operas were due to start,
(Those to be performed in August when
The company was booked to go to Edinburgh.)
But now we sang with knowledge and assurance.
Critics had reiterated former faith
In Glyndebourne standards, management was pleased,
The summer evenings mellow and the audience
Delighted with the grass as dining-table
In the two-hour dinner interval,
With the cows and nightly insects added company.
They even tolerated bats that entered
Through the scenery doors backstage – kept open
For the heat – and flew about the darkened
Auditorium, particularly in
Act IV of 'Figaro', the garden scene,
Perhaps too reminiscent of their own
For them to tell the difference.

All summer country garden evenings hold
A special magic sense of unreality,
That fragrant and elusive childhood fairyland,
Only half-remembered, but retaining,
In the deepest stronghold of subconsciousness,
A sweet intangible nostalgia that might be
Summoned up again by scents of closing flowers
Or half light fading through the trees into
A mystery of shadow and of silhouette.

To those who for the first time came from London's dust
And noise and stress to pass an evening here,
It must have been a revelation hitherto
Undreamed about. To leave a grimy station
In full evening dress – itself an odd condition
Of attendance – in the middle of a summer

Afternoon, and with three hundred others
Similarly clad, be taken by
A special train to Lewes, there to board
The fleet of buses waiting to convey them
Effortlessly through the leaf-encloistered byways
To this unsuspected haven; here to wander
Through the grounds till it was time for bells
To summon them to Mozart's shrine; and from
The nearby dressing-rooms, to hear the varied voices
Warming up for the performance with
A floating phrase or falling scale, or scintillating
High arpeggio until the notes ran smooth
And even, balanced as a string of pearls,
Identical, cascading like a waterfall;
And later, in the interval, to leave the theatre
With the ring of voices singing in their ears,
And make their way past scented trellises,
Through arbours and across the lawns
Towards their own small chosen patch of grass,
Where they would sit and sample all the sweet
And savoury delights inside Pandora's
Picnic box. The sound of merry voices
And the subtle clink of glass would float up
From each hidden niche and corner, till it seemed
The garden had become a corporate
And living entity descended on
By laughing gods. Each evening in the interval
We used to watch the pageantry of colour
Pass below the window of the Green Room,
(Where the artists ate and drank their own refreshment
Still in costume and in make-up, therefore
Not allowed to join the audience outside),
The women in their floating evening dresses
Strolling with their dark-clad escorts on the grass,
Or up the steps to disappear into the house
Itself, and there to pause inside the Organ Room

And to inspect its sombre gracious beauty.
Above the gentle babel of the passing crowd,
The faint staccato click of croquet balls
Upon the peaceful hedged-in lawn was clear
And unmistakable; and to this day
I still can visualise the R.P.O.
In evening dress, impeccable and debonair,
Engrossed in solemn and Victorian battle
With each other, blithely unaware
Of comment or advice from passers-by,
Discouraging the smallest interruption
By their dedicated and absorbed demeanour.

The bells had sounded for the second half
Of the performance. Suddenly the grounds
Were empty, cushions, rugs and picnic baskets
Stowed away once more into the cars
That slept in peaceful hundreds in their hillside
Park, waiting for their owners to return.
And while Susanna and her Figaro, the Countess
And her errant lord, the page and Barbarina
And the rest of all the characters
Entangled in the mesh of intrigue, were
At last emerging into their exquisite
Final soft ensemble, so outside, the birds,
Replete with picnic delicacies found
Upon the grass, grew silent in the trees,
And cows no longer graced the nearby hill.

(v)

Night brings its own nostalgia at the end,
Amid the long, enthusiastic flutter
Of applause, the cheering and the bows,
The flowers and smiles; and then the curtain down,
The theatre emptied of its audience –

Some to board the waiting charabancs,
Others who had come by car, to spill
Into the covered way and there to take
A last cool drink before the late drive home,
Lingering, reluctant to return
To former life of wishes and desires
Left unfulfilled, and Time an endless tyrant
At their elbow. Sad were they to leave
The beauty of that fragrant garden, now engulfed
In shadowed pools of silence, sadder still
To bid farewell to Mozart's mellow genius.
But even so, no one returns from Glyndebourne
Without accumulating something of its genial
Store of riches to commit to memory,
To treasure up with gratitude, and later on
Perhaps, to bring remembered light into
The darkness of some sombre future day.

II. UNDERSTUDY
(GLYNDEBOURNE OPERA)

(i)

Nine o'clock. Someone knocked
Hastily upon my door,
And urgency was in the voice
That summoned me.
                    'Are you awake?
You're wanted on the telephone.
They said it was important –'
Through the woolly cumulus
Of sleep the words meant nothing
Nor, until I heard the calm
And measured tones of the Administration
Secretary did I fully realise
The petrifying import of her message.
'I hope you're feeling strong,' she said,
'Because you're on to-night –
There's been an accident –
You'll have to sing Zerlina.'
I heard myself agree quite calmly
To be ready at the theatre sharp at ten
For a rehearsal, but as she rang off
Fought the impulse to return
To bed, there to continue with
This pleasant dream – (as dream, of course,
It must have been! Every understudy
Will admit it to her sleeping hours,
Sure of recognition and success.)
And then a creeping cold sensation
Overtook my consciousness
And woke me fully to what lay

A mere ten hours ahead, the ultimate
In challenges, inexorably
Inescapable.

The American soprano, who
Had sung the role so far, had been
Attacked the previous night, her handbag
Stolen and her throat too bruised
To sing. And this in Edinburgh
Where the Glyndebourne company
Had been received like royalty
By Provost and his dignitaries
As we had left the train at Waverley,
With press in flattering attendance!
To-night's performance of 'Don Giovanni'
Was almost at the season's end,
And we had sung our chorus work
For this and 'La Forza del Destino'
Each evening for several weeks
Without a break. I wished
I had been fresher vocally,
And that I had withstood
The invitation to last night's
Impromptu chamber concert,
Given by great artists
At a friendly and informal gathering
In someone's crowded house
Until the early hours.
But now was not the time to cavil
At this turn of Fortune's wheel,
So hastily I dressed, gulped down
A mere half cup of coffee, far
Too hot to finish, and then caught
The bus down to the theatre.

(ii)

It seemed I was the first
Of any understudy to be called
To sing a fairly major role;
All the music staff appeared
To have foregathered, scores in hand,
Down in the auditorium.
From ten o'clock till one I was
Put through my paces musically –
A thorough and relentless testing.
No problem there, however, for
I'd learnt the role some weeks before
The company came north, committing
It to memory on every
Train and bus to Lewes from
Victoria and back, and in
My flat reduced my friends to mute
Exasperation with persistent
Vocal repetition in my room
Until they must have known the score
As well as I.
Production was the difficulty –
Movement and stage business
Not even once rehearsed in full
Or in the proper continuity.
I had merely watched the action
From the wings – (a thousand light years
Off from doing it oneself!) – and now
Attempted to remember what went on
Upon the stage. What joy
It would have been to have sung the role
In other circumstances with
The full rehearsal period!
There seemed to be a jinx upon
This opera, for on that day

The Elvira too had fallen ill,
And so the management obtained
The services of Suzanne Danco
(Fortunately visiting
The city for her own recital.)

It was comforting to have
The willing help of Geraint Evans
As Masetto, guiding me
Wherever possible across
The stage when memory drew blank.
Don Giovanni too, full six feet five,
Italian, without much English –
(''Allo, baby – you Zerlina?
It be a' right – I 'elp.')
And so he did. So did they all,
Watchful eyes and ears alert
To catch the smallest hesitation.

(iii)

There comes a moment when all fear
Becomes irrelevant, and from then on
One almost welcomes the arrival
Of the cause of it! That evening
As the overture began,
I was beyond all other aid
Save what I had to give myself.
That endless day's rehearsal had
At least acquainted me with every
Detail, if I could remember
Sequences and timing and
The unfamiliarity
Of entrances and exits, though
Of course there was the added fear
That I would aggravate the others

[63]

By an unexpected move –
(Or lack of it!)
Standing in the crowded wings
In peasant costume, and with hair
Tied back in ribboned ringlets,
And the most ill-fitting pair of
Shoes upon my feet that I
Had ever worn, I waited, mind
As cold and clear as crystal, heart
Well stimulated by a sudden
Surge of fresh adrenalin,
And a short recurring prayer
For guidance to the Deity
Unspoken on my lips.

Then suddenly my cue had come.
No time for anything but concentration,
Every nerve alert and masking
The fatigue and the anxiety;
Masetto and the chorus giving
Their support, encouragement
And something extra for good measure;
The opening music of that scene
Already reaching out to steady
And to regulate my quickened
Pulse with all its comforting
Familiarity.... As soon as
That initial scene was over
Everyone relaxed. I even
Found myself enjoying it,
And hoped that any faulty moves
Would not disturb the well-conceived
And carefully rehearsed arrangements
For the others in the cast.
Not that it mattered, for they moved
Accordingly, responsive to

The slightest sign of wavering –
The real professionals, who hide
A crisis from their audience
And give that little more themselves
To help a newer colleague or
To cover up deficiencies.

The gods were smiling. Nothing happened
That should not have done, and though
I gave a careful rather than
Inspired performance, so at least
I had achieved what I'd been asked
To do – to make it possible
To let the curtain rise that evening.
And at the end the Maestro took
Me by the hand to take a bow
And smiled upon me kindly....
But alas, even with
Congratulations and applause,
The overwhelming feeling of
Relief was tempered by self-doubt.
Could I have given more, perhaps,
Sung with more confidence or risked
Inaccuracies to project
More of my personality,
And make a greater, more immediate
Impression?
It was left to Donna Anna,
A well-known Austrian soprano,
To put the situation into
More encouraging perspective.
'Do not reproach yourself,' she said.
'You could not have sung it better
In such circumstances. Once
I had to do the same myself.
Until you have been through a trial

Like this you do not really know
Your own potentiality.'
How right she was!
Although, since then, I've never been
Confronted with a challenge such
As that, there have been several times
When emergencies have suddenly
Arisen during a performance,
And I have subsequently found
The confidence to turn a possible
Disaster into good account.
No artist welcomes this, of course,
But all the same, to know that one
Will not give way to panic is
Additional security
In this precarious profession
We have chosen to pursue.

III. NOTHING VENTURE

How easy life must be for those
Who never stretch their hand beyond
The limits of their reach, or who accept
Those limitations all too easily
And never run the risk of danger
Or the wretchedness of failure!
What would such timid spirits know
Of such a venture as the two of us
Embarked upon? My colleague in
This experimental project was
A young composer from the States,
An excellent pianist and musician,
But, like me, unversed in business
Acumen, though what was lacking
There was more than compensated
For by faith and blind
Determination. With everything
Against us, no influence or money,
And little of what might be termed
Encouragement from anyone, we left
The safer realms of musical routine,
And resolutely turned our eyes
Towards another region. As I have said,
I was no stranger to the presentation
Of new compositions, so was well used
To swimming against the tide. Composers like
To have their works performed and will not wait
For public recognition only
At the blessing of a publisher,
So they must somehow find performers
Who can sympathise with their impatience.

Some singers may prefer to tread a safe
And well-worn path, but they will never know
How satisfying it can be
To bring a song to life at first performance.
Two works had been decided on –
A dramatic one-act opera and
A comic musical anthology
For voices and woodwind – he to write
The music, I the words, (and afterwards
To sing one of the leading roles).
In the grip of such creative
Industry, we noticed neither cool
Of spring nor summer's heat; and for
Economy we even copied all the parts
Ourselves until our eyes grew blurred
And fingers cramped, and almost we began
To wonder if we'd ever see an end
To all the hours of pen and ink.
Then at the point of near exhaustion
It was done – and had we known it –
That was when far greater troubles
Would begin!

Somehow or other we found the money,
Invited or auditioned singers
For the roles, and booked the Town Hall
Of St Pancras. Friends, and friends
Of friends, came forward to conduct, produce
And to design the costumes and
The scenery – all on a shoe-string but
With such good will and expertise
That we could not sufficiently
Express our gratitude.

For most of us it had become
A personal and monumental challenge,

And with determined singleness of purpose
And an obstinate tenacity we steered
The project to its full conclusion and
Refused to entertain the thought of failure.
Rehearsals were held in flats and rooms
And halls all over London, (and at times,
In circumstances not approved, I'm sure,
By Equity!) but soon the works took shape,
And one could see at last the final entity
Beyond the striving and the stress.

More troubles followed then at every turn, as
Everything, of course, cost so much more
Than in our innocence we'd bargained for.
Much was still missing in production, props
And costumes barely adequate, and we
Could still have done with more rehearsal.
But time for us was running out;
Our shortcomings were soon to be displayed
To public gaze and critical inspection.
Absorbed as we had been in procreation
Of our progeny, we were dismayed
To see it clothed in nothing but
The elemental threads of our simplicity.

Two pianos, for example, never will replace
An orchestra, however modest, for
An operatic presentation, but
The wind quintet for the anthology
Of 'Aesop's Fables' did full justice to
The wit and comedy of the composer's
Own intentions. The great Town Hall,
Moreover, was encouragingly full,
Though some among our audience might well
Have come from curiosity,
To satisfy themselves that such a reckless

Exploit must be doomed to failure –
(How easily do these Job's comforters
Condemn what they would never contemplate
Attempting for themselves!)
But many came that night who amply
Demonstrated their enjoyment,
And although none of the company
Became exactly famous overnight,
One could not say that it was not worth doing.
For a first essay in composition
On a larger scale, or an attempt
To launch a new-style project in a chill,
Competitive arena, it might well
Have been far worse; for we had gained a great deal
In experience – and the critics too were kind.

IV. OPERA NIGHT AT TONYPANDY

(i)

Excitement rising through the valley
Like a mist that permeates
Each crevice of the mind's anticipation
Like bubbles in an unfamiliar wine.
Weeks before the Company is due,
All who can spare the time – or manufacture it –
From less illuminating tasks, fall with enthusiasm,
Brooms and pans and cloths and polish,
Mops and pails upon the modest local hall
To furbish up its shabby, poor amenities.
Among the final hammering to bolster up
The rickety, uneven stage, the scenery arrives
In lurching lorries down the cobbled street
Like the vanguard of an army. Everyone turns out
To look and wave and comment as they pass,
The children running wild. A swift, efficient
Team reduces the ensuing chaos in the hall,
Adjusting, making do, extemporising till
The stage is set for Violetta's evening party
And her fateful meeting with Alfredo.

Early in the afternoon emerge musicians with
Their instruments, stage managers with pencilled notes;
Laden ladies of the wardrobe sidling past
The electricians rigging up the lights, and last of all
The singers, and conductor purposeful with score
And baton. Competent, unhurried, each one
Knowing his appointed place, they move
Like players on a board, to meet the deadline
For the dress rehearsal. The dressing-rooms,

[71]

Too few and far too small, cannot accommodate
With ease their occupants, and tempers soon begin to fray.
The conductor is too old and tried a hand to remonstrate
With discontent among his company; with skill
And sympathy, diplomacy and charm,
He soothes their ruffled temperaments to coax
Both power and beauty from their golden throats.
And later, miners coming from the pits
Stop to listen and to smile and nod approval
To each other as they hear these preparations
For the feast, due to begin at eight o'clock.
Housewives hasten with the evening meal
And urge their children into Sunday clothes
Long laid out clean and ready.

Rehearsal over, all disperse to rest and eat
And gather up their strength again. Forceful ladies
Of the welcoming committee, puffed up with modest pride,
(Those with a guest room in their homes!) offer hospitality
To these famed beings from another world,
Imbuing them for ever after with a reputation
Far more exalted than in fact, so that some
Of that richer radiance might reflect upon their hosts –
A reassurance to their neighbours of their wisdom
In electing *them* to serve artistic needs
Within their small community!

(ii)

Theatre in darkness, baton raised:
Behind the faded curtains singers in position
Gather themselves in final readiness
To act upon their cue;
Every corner of the auditorium is
Filled to overflowing, every eye
Expectant, centred solely on the man

At whose command the forces under his control
Will be unleashed, and music flood
Upon their waiting ears.

The curtain rises and the tiny stage,
Ablaze with colour, light and movement,
Sets nerves and breathing quickening in response.
The singers too are soon aware of this rapport;
No smart bejewelled audience
At Covent Garden or the Wells
Would follow every phrase and nuance
Of the voices with such passionate attention,
Such understanding and commiseration
With ill-fated Violetta.
(How well they know their 'Traviata' in this valley!)

Now all the former tensions and fatigue
Of travel and rehearsal under difficult conditions,
The irritation at the lack of space,
The thick, ill-ventilated atmosphere,
The extra care they have to take
In order not to step upon each other's dresses
As they move, the dangers both to life and limb
Behind the scenes – all this
Is now forgotten, and the cast,
Professional, assured and competent,
Have settled happily into their stride;
Ear and larynx both respond to former years
Of training, and they sing directly to
The hearts of all their listeners –
Not only those inside the theatre who are there
Legitimately, having paid for tickets, but
The other larger audience outside, packed closely round
Its wooden walls, their eyes glued to the cracks between
The thin uneven planks, their breathing quiet in order
Not to miss a note. For even up the village street

[74]

It was still possible to hear, and several hundred
Stood or sat, transfixed and silent in a trance
Of pleasure and fulfilment. (How well they love
Their Verdi in this valley!)
And after the magnificent dénouement
Of Violetta's painful gathering of new found strength,
Her last asseveration of her former health
Before her final fall, there is a silence
So profound it seems as if the hundreds there
Are turned to living stone, so still are they,
Acceptance of the tragedy not yet upon them.

(iii)

Three hours only, yet infinity
Between the time before and that to follow!
A glimpse into a life so different
And dramatic that it moves them almost bodily
Out of their own true time and place,
And lingers on the retina of eye and mind.

The tumult of applause and shouting,
Autographs, congratulations
Are already in the past;
The weary artists are at last
Once more themselves. They and the orchestra,
Their minds projected forward to
Their next appointment with the Muse,
Emerge into the freshening night and fill
Their grateful lungs with moonlit air.

At first the crowd, with mind's eye still aglow
With riches to be stored against the greyer days,
Are still unwilling to begin the homeward trudge;
Huddled close together, they discuss
With rapid lilt and emphasis the highlights

And the merits of performance.
But soon at last excitement ebbs
Into contentment, and a stream
Of footsteps echo up the cobbled street,
Diminishing in size and sound
Like pebbles on a falling tide.
To-morrow some of them will tramp
These weary miles again for 'Rigoletto'.
Never mind the aching feet, the spirit
Is uplifted and recharged!
And now and then some other voices will renew,
In gold and silver harmony, the spell
And the enchantment of a well-remembered phrase
And send it winging through the slowly deepening night,
To set the sleeping valleys ringing to
The joyful echo of their natural heritage.

V. 'OH HEART, MELT IN WEEPING!'

The Passion of Our Lord according to St John.
Last night I sang those two great arias again,
And found their impact still as strong as ever.
Not a phrase was staled by repetition,
Not a note or word seemed false or out of place.
After flights of lyric freedoms that make
All emotion seem mere mawkish sentiment,
Or adventurous excursions to the outer
Limits of contemporary mode,
It was a special joy to find myself once more
Confined within the sterner disciplines of Bach:
To feel, as on my first acquaintance with the score,
That same delight, astonishment and wonder in
The clear and balanced structure of design
That scorns the dubious devices used by
Less inventive minds, and lets the intricate
Simplicity speak for itself; and in his clarity
Of counterpart within a strict convention,
That invests the bitterest of sorrow with
An equal passion and detachment.

This work, and others, I remember having learnt
Throughout a grey, unhappy summer full of rain
And desolate emotion, in the stillness of
A tiny country church, where I was certain
To be undisturbed for hours of the day.
Alone, save for the silent pageantry
Of passing ghosts within the crevices
Of ancient stone, the dark oppression
Of my circumstance gave way

[77]

Before the greater agonies and sorrows
Of the score; and then – as now – within
The tender arias and gravely beautiful chorales,
I found a new fulfilment and serenity.

VI. LESSON WITH MADAME 'X'

Long had I admired her work,
Her voice and her musicianship.
Worldwide acclaim for her achievements
Having led to honours being
Offered and accepted, she became
A teacher, taking as her pupils
Young professionals or students
Sufficiently advanced as to be
Interesting. I wrote and told her
All that I had done so far,
And that I would be grateful for
Advice on certain aspects of
Her repertoire. Would she take me?
Yes, she would, on Tuesday next
At three o'clock to be precise,
And bring my own accompanist.

My usual pianist was away,
So I arranged to bring with me
Another who was quite intrigued
To meet this famous lady.
He was a sensitive and gentle
Soul, and sympathetic to
His soloists. We worked at several
Operatic arias,
And on the day appointed,
Full of bright anticipation,
We were shown into her presence.

She was not tall and certainly
No longer young, but there was still

About her an impressive strength,
A strange magnetic quality
Both attractive and disturbing.
Here was a personality
Stamped with the hallmark of success,
Whose vigour and vitality
Bespoke a fiercely resolute
Determination, blinding her
To failure or defeat. No doubts
Or hesitancy here, nothing
That would mar her progress
To her chosen goal.

I caught my pianist's eye and saw
My sudden trepidation mirrored there.
He too had read a certain challenge
In this lady's eye. It seemed we were
To have a test as thorough and severe
As any big audition.

She sat apart beside the window
Intimating with a nod
That we were to begin. At first
She listened most attentively,
Her hazel eyes fixed piercingly
Upon my face, but all at once
The music took her in its hold
And smiling, she was on her feet
And with her arm began to beat
A wild erratic rhythm which
Soon led us through a labyrinth
Of inexplicable rubato,
Taking baffling liberties
With Bizet's score and making it
Almost impossible to follow.

At the end we waited, silent,
Far from certain of the outcome,
Half expecting a dismissal
For a tentative performance.
I was relieved when she invited me
To sing again. And then began
The strangest moments of a very
Strange and disconcerting afternoon.
As each aria followed on the next,
Madame 'X's critical
Enthusiasm grew. We stood there
Almost face to face while she,
With flashing eyes that saw not me,
But some vast audience of former time,
Made gestures of encouragement
And emphasis with total disregard
For those directions in the score;
And at each dénouement she would join in
Herself   her voice still strong and true,
Remarkable in beauty for her age –
But making it impossible,
Of course, for her to hear a note
Of what I sang. And then
She turned her full attention on
My struggling accompanist
Who, baffled by conflicting
Soloists, had tried to please
The one without endangering
The other, all to no avail.
It was clear that Madame 'X'
Was not entirely pleased with his performance,
For she frowned, and without warning
Smote him smartly on the shoulder.
'You! Whatever your name is – !
You must *never* leave your singer
High and dry when she goes above the stave!

She needs support, so you must play
As if you were the orchestra!'

I dared not look at him, but sensed
The shock and outrage breaking through
His gentle outer shell. He had not winced
At her uncivil treatment, but
He now resumed his playing with
A strength and brilliance that almost
Drowned my ending of the aria.
She had not meant to hurt, of course.
In the excitement of the moment
Her mercurial temperament
Had carried her beyond control;
But now she bore him no ill-will, and
Said that she would hear one more.

'Depuis le Jour' had always been
A favourite of mine, and I
Had sung it with success on numerous
Occasions. Alas, my voice was not enough
To satisfy my listener, for
Again she joined me in competitive
Duet, and just before the end
Decided that my mouth was not
Sufficiently wide open. So
To demonstrate her point, before
I realised her full intention,
She approached and tapped me sharply
On the cheek, adjuring me
To follow her example as she sang.

Here again no malice was intended.
Her vehement enthusiasm
Merely found expression in

Whatever action seemed to her
Appropriate, but as for me,
It was not just the stinging pain
Of that swift blow that made the tears
Spring to my eyes (for these were just
The logical result); far more than that,
My disbelief and disappointment
Tightened up my throat against my voice,
And for the moment I was speechless.

Somehow we finished off the piece, then in
Unspoken, mutual agreement
Took our leave with dignity, without
Recrimination or regret,
In both our minds the puzzled thought –
How could one possibly equate
That melting fire and loveliness
That once had been her voice, with this
Incredible and blind insensitivity?
All I had done was to approach
The shrine of her accumulated
Knowledge and experience,
To seek in all humility
And eagerness to share its riches.
Sadly these had been denied me
Through her inability
To subjugate herself and all
The glories of her past beneath
The greater glory of the music
She had lived to serve.

The operas we sing are not
Our personal possessions, stamped
With all the subtle facets of
Our own performance, patented

And laid down like a blueprint for
The future use and guidance
Of a younger generation.
That is to deny the essence
And the genius of the mind
That gave them being, to relegate them
To a secondhand commodity.

So this, I knew, was not for me.
I wrote declining her kind offer
To take me as a pupil, and received
A card that left me in no doubt
That my decision had been wise.
As for my pianist, the buffeting
Which he received has left a guarded
Wariness where prima donnas
Are concerned. Next time, I feel,
There will be more than hint of steel
In his response to bludgeoning.
And yet, like me, he understood
What motivation lay behind
Her rough uncouth behaviour. The ending
To an era of success has to be faced
By every artist soon or late –
And singers suffer most of all,
For voices last a shorter time.
To hear with patience and forbearance
The attempts of others to achieve
The heights that one has occupied
In splendour for so many years,
Is not what everyone can bear
With equanimity or gentleness:
And for a personality as strong
As hers, as forceful and imperious,
It must at times have been beyond
The limits of endurance.

However, it was an experience
Not soon to be forgotten, and although
In one way it would leave its mark,
In another, we had understood,
Could still admire, and so forgive.

VII. CHRISTOPHE COLOMB

(i)

Among the regular routine of oratorio,
Chamber music concerts or recitals for
Varieties of music clubs, in halls and churches,
Drawing-rooms and stately homes, occasionally
There comes another kind of musical engagement
Which, though not for solo work, great kudos or
Enormous fee, is none the less acceptable
For its unusual interest. Such was Claudel's play
'Christophe Colomb' with music by Darius Milhaud,
To be presented at the Palace Theatre, London,
By Jean-Louis Barrault and Madeleine Renaud,
His wife, together with their enterprising
Company from France. The music was to be
Directed by a young and highly talented
Conductor new to English audiences. His name
Was Pierre Boulez, an unassuming, sensitive
Musician who identified himself and his
Small chamber group with Milhaud's musical intentions
So that they were immediately coherent and
Effective to interpret. It was soon made clear
To us – the singers – that we were to take an active
Part throughout the play, even mingling now
And then with actors on the stage, and to this end
We were attired in monkish garb – long robe and cowl,
And made to sit upon the shallow steps that led
From stage to pit behind the instrumentalists.
We went through most intensive sessions of rehearsal,
For which I found myself interpreter, for our
Conductor spoke so little English that
Communication might have been a difficulty.

[86]

The company arrived the day before we opened,
And from thenceforth the set was inundated with
Stage management and staff, and wardrobe mistresses
Distractedly attempting to discuss their urgent
Business with the actors and the actresses,
While they in turn were occupied in running through
Their sole rehearsal in these new surroundings.
Everywhere a frenzied pandemonium
Of routine chaos spread across the crowded stage
To the complete and total unconcern
Of Jean-Louis Barrault himself. No matter what
The problem, he would deal with it efficiently,
His aquiline and high-bridged nose with flaring nostrils,
Intelligent and piercing eyes beneath the high
Commanding forehead, giving him the air
Of hawk among the pigeons. Even when
The details of direction were decided and
The singers had been taken through their forays on
The stage, the company continued to rehearse,
Sotto voce, but with actions, till the final
Moment – about an hour or so before
The theatre doors would open to the public.

(iii)

Miraculously, by the time that they were due
To take up their positions on the stage,
The tired actors had thrown off exhaustion, and we
Gathered round Monsieur Barrault, who spoke a short
And pithy homily in French, adjuring all
The company to rise to the occasion and
To give a wonderful performance: 'Très fort
Et très virile!' he ended, adding with a flashing
Smile to us, in case we had not understood:

[87]

'Vairy strong! Vairy tough!'
And suddenly the evening temperature was rising
To performance level, and the heady First Night
Atmosphere descended on us all. To work
Again inside a theatre, even in ensemble,
Was both stimulating and rewarding,
Particularly with a musical director
Such as ours, who steered his minute orchestra
So capably through all the hazards of the score,
Watchful eye and hand upon each vocal entry,
Gathering together all the final threads
Of sound from every quarter when the singers rose
To join the actors on the vast and lofty stage.

Although in French, 'Christophe Colomb' held audience
And critics bound in silence and absorbed in
Satisfaction and delight – a beautiful
And strange concoction of true theatre qualities.
Throughout, both Madeleine Renaud and Jean-Louis
More than justified their most illustrious
Reputation, the melting beauty of her own
Performance matched against the fiery strength of his;
While all the rest of us concerned in it conspired
With Milhaud to enhance and emphasise the drama,
Adding depth and lustre to the text as if
Illumined by a fierce intensity of inner light.

THIRD MOVEMENT

(In moto perpetuo, ma senza rigore)

I. PIERROT LUNAIRE

Embalmed in comfort in the great express
Now roaring northward to the Scottish capital,
I noticed we were stealthily accompanied
By snowflakes gathering in density
The further we progressed along the route.
I shuddered at the thought of spending several days
In such unpleasant weather, and particularly
At the moment, for I was not really well.
I had been singing with the Grosvenor Ensemble,
(A group comprising solo voices and
A wind quintet), and we had just presented
At the Purcell Room five first performances
Of works by different composers. Naturally,
This had entailed a great deal of rehearsal,
Making heavier demands upon the vocal
Stamina than had been usual formerly.
Several of us had caught colds, and I was still
Uncomfortably aware that mine at least
Had not entirely left me. There were signs
Of sudden lack of that response my voice
Would normally have made to my demands,
And there were still to come the five performances
Of Schoenberg's most demanding work 'Pierrot Lunaire',
(To which the Ballet Rambert would be dancing
At the Royal Lyceum in Edinburgh.) For this,
A mere four busy crowded weeks before,
I had been booked as the reciter. Little wonder
That I sat with head immersed inside
The Schoenberg score, and hoped my voice would stay the
    course.

The part for solo speaker had to be declaimed
In intricate and difficult cross-rhythms, using
All the voice throughout its range, but in the style
Of 'sprechgesang', or 'singing-speech', more tiring
To a singer than long hours of actual singing.
I at first had found it an elusive work
To learn in its atonal idiom,
But fascinating all the same, and not so far
Removed from some of the new works we were
About to sing in London.

(ii)

I stayed with Scottish cousins who were understanding,
Kind and patient, leaving me in peace to study.
Outside, the cold was paralysing. Hitherto
My visits to the city had been made in summer
With the Glyndebourne company, but now I found it
Difficult to recognise the place! The length of
Princes Street a white and chilling vista
Down which both traffic and pedestrians progressed
With extra care beneath a waste of ice-pale sky;
While sound itself seemed stifled in the cold still air
That hurt the lungs and penetrated to the bones.

The Royal Lyceum Theatre was old-fashioned,
High and spaciously designed, although
In weather such as this not warm enough for comfort.
There was one area, however, – the dancers'
Dressing-rooms – where heat had been maintained,
An integral necessity for muscles stiffened
By the journey through the frozen streets.
I was assigned to one such room and thawed out
Thankfully among the limbering dancers.

[92]

The pit from which the instrumentalists and I
Were to accompany the ballet suffered
From a searing draught that sought our shrinking feet
And fingers, till I nearly lost all contact
With extremities and found the turning of
A page an unexpected hazard. Here the players
Fared much better since they were more busily
Employed, with piano keys or wind or strings
To be manipulated.

(iii)

As at the Mercury we faced familiar problems.
'Pierrot Lunaire' is difficult enough to play
Or to recite, without the added need to follow
A conductor's beat in turn subjected now
And then to tempi variations for the dancers'
Benefit. Not for us the luxury
Of adaptation merely to the interplay
Between each colleague and composer's score.
Our tempo was subsidiary to dancer's style,
To height of leap and force of gravity,
And if we did not watch the beat most carefully
Ensemble would inevitably suffer.
The work, however, easily transcribed itself
Into balletic terms and clarified the vivid
German text. 'Pierrot', the traditional
'Commedia dell' Arte' figure, wanders through
A moonlit landscape into weird extensions of
His fevered and moonstruck imagination – nightmare
Sequences of terror and of violence
Interlaced with welcome threads of humour,
Though fantastic and grotesque, but touchingly
Depicted by the choreography;
Most of this was centred round a high
And leafy structure on the stage,

[93]

And dancers climbed all over and around it
In a scheme of movement startling in
Conception and originality.

Even with the utmost care, it was not always
Possible for words to penetrate
The texture of the instrumental playing;
Therefore, listened to without the action of
The dancers, it would need a detailed translation
Of the poems to appreciate in full
The striking, jagged brilliance of the score.
Tiring it most certainly became towards
The last of these performances, and furthermore,
The weather had not helped to heal the ravages
Of previous infection in my throat.
Between performances I hardly spoke a word
And generally behaved as laymen tend to think
All singers do throughout their lives – avoiding draughts
By crouching, muffled to the ears in wool and fur,
Beside whatever source of warmth was then available.

When it was over I began to feel
Distinctly strange, as if impelled by unseen hands
To take my leave next day and board the train
To London, almost unaware of what
I said or did, without volition or
A sense of any clear direction. All I knew
Was that I had to be in London early on
The following day for a rehearsal for the next
Recital at the Purcell Room, also by
The Grosvenor Ensemble, involving once again
Performances of four new works both difficult
And taxing for the voice. There was nothing else
To do but yet again immerse my aching head
In yet another fearsome score, ignore
The icy world outside and try to concentrate
On more immediate priorities.

[94]

II. INFLUENZA OBBLIGATO

(i)

Reason, commonsense and caution
Argued fiercely for withdrawal
From this concert at the Purcell Room,
Although I had survived rehearsal
With the Grosvenor Ensemble
Upon the previous day,
And no one in the group had
Guessed my actual condition.
Had this been oratorio,
Involving standard repertoire,
Or even a recital on my own,
There would have been no other course
But to have opted out from the performance
Immediately my symptoms
Had become so feverish.
No problem there to find
A substitute soprano who
Already knew the work, or
Even another singer to have filled
The gap with a different
Recital programme.
I could have then retired
To bed in reach of medicines
And doctors, and succumbed
In comfort to the ravages
Of this unpleasant virus.

There was a snag, however;
Four new compositions –
Two distinctly classifiable

As 'avant garde' –
Are not so easily performed
By someone who has seen
The scores less than
Two days before the concert.
Even if we could have found
An excellent sight-reader –
Preferably with perfect pitch –
Who would have been available
To have rehearsed non-stop,
The others in the group
Were seldom free of concert work,
And needed days of warning
In advance, in any case,
To get together for rehearsal.
Since to cancel the performance
Would have meant enormous losses
To the management and since,
Surprisingly, my voice appeared
To be still with me,
I decided to abandon
Further doubts, and somehow
To hang on throughout the evening.

The run-through in the morning
At the Purcell Room
Had gone quite well –
At least, we felt that there was
Little more that could be done
In such a short rehearsal time
As we had had at our disposal.
Concentration was the one
Key-factor for success, to count
Consistently and hope
That pitch at awkward entries
Would be accurate. How often

Had I wished that I'd been blessed
With perfect pitch! Relative
Pitch, however good, remains
Still relative to other notes;
No need to worry just
As long as these are accurate
Or – and equally important –
Even if they *are*, that
You can *hear* them in the
Dissonant miasma floating
Past your straining ears.

(ii)
I had not dared
To take my temperature
Before we struggled once again
Across the treacherous, icy roads,
To gather at the Purcell Room
That evening to change.
Dosed with remedies
To keep me on my feet,
My natural optimism
Reassured me of survival
Till the end at half-past nine.
After that it did not matter,
For I had a welcome break
Of several weeks without engagement,
So could vanish
Without let or hindrance
From the concert scene
And so to bed.
(That beckoning image had to be
Most brutally suppressed.
Not yet for me the craved release,
Relinquishing my aching bones

[97]

Into those fathomed depths
Of luxury!)
At seven thirty we were ready
In the Green Room, garbed
In evening dress, white ties and tails,
Spruced and perfumed, debonair,
With instruments in tune
And voices warmed up once again,
Those awkward passages gone over
Finally for safety's sake.

But now a curious, unreal
Sensation had enveloped me.
It was as if another person
Stood there in my place,
While I was floating effortlessly
In the air beside her,
Aware that she was suffering
In head and throat and eyes
(That flinched behind
Her contact lenses),
Yet free myself of any
Feeling whatsoever.
I knew her pulse was throbbing
At a rate that must have
Shaken her, but heard her singing
Quite correctly, saw her watching
The conductor's baton, recognised
The strange, yet so familiar,
Progressions weaving through
The wind quintet's accompaniment,
And then the first wave of applause.
And so it went throughout the evening,
Entries, exits, smiling,
Bowing, always with the floor
A little way below my feet,

Floating by my alter ego,
Near, yet at a light year's
Distance. (Perhaps this strange
Detachment presaged death,
I did not care, but clung
Tenaciously to waning
Sense and self-control.)

(iii)

How inexplicably will memory
Co-operate when under stress!
Vocal, aural, muscular –
Each of these three faculties
Had accurately reproduced
My part in these new works
Without the active instigation
Of my conscious mind.
In fact, I had no recollection
Of that evening's end,
Although it must have been successful,
For afterwards the critics were
Remarkably encouraging.
In retrospect, of course,
One cannot help but wonder
If this sort of risk
Is worth the cost, but at the time
It seems to be inevitable
And there can be no choice.
Others when hard-pressed
No doubt have done the same
In what they felt to be good cause.
I overstepped the safety line
And paid for it, for by the time
Both health and sanity returned,
The snow and ice had melted
And the crocuses had come.

III. NOCTURNE

The beautiful old house in which the concert
Would be held stood in another century,
Placid in perpetuation, uninvaded
By the crass intrusion of the present day,
Its gentle dignity reflecting generations
Of a peaceful and contented occupation.
Happiness was paramount, permeating
The residual tensions and the stress
Indigenous to our profession, and
Instinctively we found ourselves responding
To the balm of its serenity.

We had taken time and care to build a programme
Suitable for such surroundings. Arias
By Mozart, groups of Fauré and Duparc,
Were interspersed with clarinet and piano pieces,
Ending with my favourite work of Schubert for
The three of us – 'The Shepherd on the Rock'.

Outside, the varied scents of summer mingled with
The smell of polished wood and bowls of roses and
Gypsophila inside the spacious music room.
From where I sang, I faced the tall French windows
Opened wide on to the terrace where the broad
And shallow steps led down on to the lawn,
And noticed how the fading light was subtly
Altering the colours of the garden –
Black-green yew and ilex merging in
A multiplicity of swaying shadows,
Points of silver light upon the gathering dew,
And everywhere a slowly deepening silence.

Fauré's beautiful 'Nocturne', and 'Nell',
'Après un Rêve', and 'Ici-bas' seemed singularly
Apt for this douce evening, while in his exquisite
'Clair de Lune' it was not difficult
To conjure up the charming 'masques et bergamasques'
Moving in their grave and graceful minuet
Upon the grass, while svelte and slender fountains
Wept in ecstasy beside still marble figures
In the calm, sad beauty of the moonlight.

Happy is the artist when he knows
He has approached the shining edge
Of his particular perfection!
To feel he has achieved the final union
Of harmony and balance in his art is rare,
For seldom are performers satisfied
With all the facets of their execution.

But sometimes – unexpectedly – you have a glimpse
Of what you have been striving for, and then –
Like stepping out from shade into the sun –
The curtains part upon the golden rubicon,
And everything that you have ever done before
Is only preparation. Such a moment
Came, I think, to all of us that evening
In that atmosphere of grace and of repose,
Our minds in tune, peculiarly tranquil
And receptive, able to create a new
Dimension to the music, and award
Ourselves the rare encouragement of knowing
We had earned our momentary accolade.

IV. BURGH HOUSE IN WINTER

(i)

Baroque music in a charming setting,
Elegance the keynote –
This at least was the intention
Of our new-formed trio
For a concert
In a Hampstead venue.
Burgh House had been chosen,
Booked and our publicity
Distributed, and everything
Rehearsed to concert pitch
All ready for performance.
All, that is, except for factor 'x' –
Which, like unpredictable,
Avenging Nemesis, crept up
To cause a deadly combination
Of events, exacerbating
A potentially explosive
Situation. Sudden bitter
Weather with sub-freezing
Temperatures, on top of
The already widespread
Strikes and union confrontations
With the government, resulted
In the country shivering
Through regular protracted cuts
In electricity. Concerts
Far and wide were cancelled, causing
Irretrievable and serious loss
To artists and to managements alike.

However, soon a three-hour cut
Was introduced at three-hour intervals,
And managements worked miracles
Of making do with minimums
To meet their concert schedules.
We had been assured that light
And warmth would be available
Inside Burgh House from six p.m. till nine
Upon the evening of the concert.
This would give sufficient time
For the performance, so,
As we were all indigenous
To Britain – thus innured
To variations in
Her meteorological domain –
We agreed to risk it,
Since to cancel everything
So late might mean an audience
Arriving at an empty hall.

(ii)

We had finally arranged
For the arrival of the harpsichord
At six o'clock, allowing
Time for tuning and a
Short rehearsal afterwards.
But when we reached the gates,
There seemed to be some sort
Of trouble and commotion
Further down the street,
With people and police all
Mingled on the pavement
Amid a general air
Of worry and anxiety.
We heard mention of

A robbery – and suddenly
I felt the clammy hand
Of some impending retribution
On my shrinking shoulder.
Somewhere the Fates were laughing,
Throwing the callous weight
Of their disdain and mockery
Against us – nor was I mistaken.
Alas for plans of mice and men!
Burgh House was swathed in silent
Darkness and a stark,
Consolidated cold
That bit into the soul
To leave its numbing mark
Upon eternity.
Something had gone wrong,
And there had been no heat
Or light since yesterday,
So the caretaker informed us.
Chilled beyond apology,
He obviously hoped that we
Would disappear as quickly
As we'd come, and none
Be any wiser. Useless
To recriminate,
Or to apportion blame
At this late hour.

We held a hurried conclave with
Disaster, doom and darkness
Facing us, decided we must wait
And see if anyone turned up,
Devoutly hoping that the night
Was too unpleasant to attract
The music lovers of the district!
For safety's sake, the harpsichord

Was tuned and tested by the light
Of lamps and torches balanced
On the music stands.
(Throughout this wretched period
Of heat and lighting vagaries,
Most people armed themselves with torches,
Caravan and other lamps,
And we were well equipped in this direction.)
We lit the foyer and the hall
With a dim and ghostly light,
And shrouded in thick overcoats
And scarves, voice and recorder
Tremulously tried out the
Acoustics, breath congealing
Into vapour seconds
After its emission.
We were due to start at seven,
But by twenty minutes to
No one had come, to our relief.
Visions of home comfort rose up
Tantalisingly to tempt us
To withdraw; in fact, we were
Beginning to dismantle
The equipment when
Some visitors arrived
And stood amazed in semi-darkness,
Till their eyes became
Accustomed to the gloom
And they were able to
Approach and ask for tickets.
Five minutes to, and there were now
More than a score of muffled figures
Huddled closely in their seats,
Strangely cheerful, blatantly
Expectant of an evening's entertainment.
Having battled through

The adverse elements, nothing
And nobody would deter them
From their due. Theirs was the final
Victory and ours the chilling
Task of justifying it.

(iii)

It was the only time that I had ever sung
In evening dress, fur coat and boots,
Shuddering my way through Purcell's
'Blessed Virgin's Expostulation',
Every run and trill quadrupled
By my constant shivering.

A fleeting thought now passed
Unbidden through my mind
Of what incongruous and quite
Extraordinary spectacle
We must present, and for
A sudden, stricken moment
I fell victim to
A totally unwarranted
Hilarity, and dared not
Turn my eyes towards
The nearby shadowed harpsichord
Played by a swaddled figure
Hunched above his shaking,
Scarlet-mittened fingers,
For an urge to laugh just then
Would have set up permanent
Vibration in my diaphragm.
The pitch of the recorder too
Was slightly flattened by the cold,
And in the following ensemble
All three of us were struggling to

[106]

Adjust ourselves to these conditions
Unobtrusively, to keep
Our gallant audience in happy
Ignorance of the extent
Of all our difficulties.
'Oh God!' I prayed towards the end,
'Make them go home when we have
Finished this!' But there
The stalwart stoics stayed
To give us their encouragement –
The British way of rising in
The face of dire adversity! –
And smiled with stiffened lips upon
This frozen igloo of our discontent.

The applause that greeted every item
Gratified us by its length
And its ferocity, although,
Of course, we realised that
Since the circulation has
To be maintained somehow,
This was the most polite
And obvious way of doing it!

We reached the interval at last,
And hopefully the organiser
Made a speech of welcome,
Intimating that no one
Would mind or feel in any way
Rejected should the audience
Decide that they had now endured
Enough discomfort for one evening –
Their money too would be refunded.
This was scornfully refused,
And he was cheerfully assured

That they were all enjoying it
And would we please continue?

After that, there was no more to say.
Artists and audience, as with one mind,
Decamped along the road into
The nearest licensed premises,
And in the next ten minutes,
In its candled and congenial warmth,
We joined in breaking
Every known artistic rule
By swallowing a brimming glass –
Or was it two perhaps? –
Of some rum punch concoction,
Hot and strong enough to melt
The glaciers of long-forgotten time....

(iv)

The blood once more began to flow,
Coursing through our sluggish arteries,
And colouring the hitherto grey evening
With the orange-molten glow
Of hot Jamaican sun.
A hint of festival crept into
The behaviour of our audience,
Who clearly felt that they
Had gained ascendancy
Over sordid circumstance;
And once resettled in their seats they
Generated sweet, rum-flavoured warmth
Into the dim and chilly atmosphere.
My voice miraculously answered
My directions, the recorder too
Was now mellifluously back in tune,
And those once shaking fingers

On the harpsichord
Gave accurate account of solo
Or ensemble or accompaniment.

I suppose most artists must have suffered
Similar experience at one time
Or another, maybe in those
Icy church performances
Of oratorio, but never, we maintain,
In conditions quite as bad as ours
Upon that freezing February night;
Nor found such valiant audience
Which, having come upon disaster,
Gallantly remained,
Endured, applauded and sustained
Three artists in extremity.

V. OCTOBER IN PARIS

(i)

Whether in October or the Spring,
The charm of Paris never falters or
Grows stale for me, even with the fierce
Congestion of its traffic and tired tempers
Of its drivers. That which we detest
In central London is acceptable
In Paris for a host of other reasons.
Tired though I was on my arrival, having
Sung the night before in Strasbourg, still
I could appreciate the luxury
Of travel in the famous 'T.E.E.',
(Trans-European Express) to Paris, with
Its automated doors and carpeted
Compartments, and the courtesy of its
Loudspeaker system to advise
The passengers of its amenities,
Or give them warning of its imminent
Arrival at their destination.

Paris was as I remembered it
From former visits, bright with midday sun,
Its citizens foregathering upon
The pavement cafés to partake
Of their aperitifs or déjeuner,
The air alive with uninhibited
And cheerful voices. (Why are we in England
So restrained in our enjoyment?)
                                    I was due
To meet the other members of the chamber
Music group for lunch before we went

EROICA CHAMBER GROUP

Anthony Worsdell
(*Clarinet*)

Roxane Houston
(*Soprano*)

Margaret Moncrieff
(*Cello*)

Michael Hobson
(*Composer and Pianist*)

To our rehearsal for the concert at
The 'Cercle Interallié' that evening.
They had flown from London earlier
That morning, (oboe, cello, flute and pianist),
And were more than ready, as was I,
To sample the delicious lunch provided
By the thoughtful organisers at
A nearby restaurant, a fitting prelude
To the sort of evening every artist
Dreams about but seldom will experience.

None of us had ever played or sung
In such surroundings as this beautiful
High-ceilinged room, an eighteenth-century salon,
Perfectly proportioned, with its graceful
Air of fragile elegance still
Undisturbed by present day intrusion.
Candlelight was lacking, but the modern
Lighting was discreetly placed, and any
Renovations cleverly disguised.
The salon held about two hundred chairs –
Louis XV – white and gilt, with brilliant blue
Upholstery in contrast to the crimson
Velvet of the curtains, while the ceiling
Was enlivened by exquisite paintings
Edged with frames embossed in cream and gold.
Our first impressions were of light and space,
And flattering acoustics which were not
Too resonant despite the polished wooden
Floors and ornate mirrored walls. The platform
At one end accommodated all
Of us quite easily, and led down several
Steps into another smaller room
Of equal grace and beauty, delegated
For the artists' special use.

[112]

We had been asked to give a programme that
Was light and not too serious, so we
Had chosen some of our most popular
And best-known pieces, adding to the ease
And general enjoyment of
The evening. There was only one short moment
Of alarm when two of the ensemble
Did not reach the 'Cercle Interallié'
Until a mere five minutes in advance
Of when we were to start. Having gone
To change at their hotel, they had misjudged
The time that it would take them to return
Through such congested streets. The organisers
Had become a little restive and
Uneasy, understandably, for almost
Every chair inside the salon was now
Occupied; but soon the errant artists
Re-appeared, regained their breath, and we
Began one of the easiest and most
Delightful evening's work that ever came our way.

(ii)

How unexpected and how gratifying
To be greeted by an audience clad
In full regalia! – bejewelled and scented
Ladies, chic and colourful in satin
And brocade, the gentlemen more soberly
Attired with medals on their dark lapels,
And over all an air of festival
In unimpeachable good taste –
The unmistakable ingredients for
A glamorous and glittering occasion!
Under such encouraging conditions
Every artist will respond like plant
To summer sun, and we were no exception.

[113]

It was clear our audience appreciated
The immediate attraction of
The varied pieces we had chosen.
Paul Genin's 'Carnival of Venice' – (that
Absurd, delicious tune for the piano,
Taken over and improved upon
By flute in devastating variations),
Demanded – and received – fantastic
Virtuosity, and drew much laughter
And a cheer; and Fauré's 'Elégie'
For cello held the listeners in thrall.
My songs were mostly French, some solo with
Piano, others early arias accompanied
By oboe or by flute, all tuneful and
Ingratiating to the ear. I ended
With a folksong from the Haute Auvergne,
Sung in the local patois, (which required
Some explanation for the benefit
Of this Anglo-French community).
This song, about a self-important
Quail, diverted and amused them all.

When it was over, and the audience
Had shown its pleasure and approval, we
Were bidden to attend a small reception
In a nearby room, to meet some of the
Organising team and other guests.
We said we'd be enchanted, and obeyed.
By now no one would have been surprised
If they had offered us a splendid five-course
Dinner in the company of thirty
Other guests at least – and this, of course,
Was just exactly what they did! After
Champagne in the anteroom, and graceful
Compliments and comments on the merit
Of the concert, we adjourned with our

Attentive hosts to yet another larger
Room set out with separate tables, there to
Do unbridled justice to a menu
Of unparalleled delight
And ingenuity. My neighbour chose
A brace of garnished quail, solemnly
Assuring me that neither was the one
That I had mentioned in my song! But though
Superbly cooked, I could not bring myself
To eat that dish, so chose another not so
Reminiscent of a former friend!

After such frivolity as this
It was impossible, of course, to come back
Down to earth and more mundane engagements
All at once, and it was fully several months,
I'm sure, before my colleagues ceased to feel,
As I did, that no evening concert was
Complete without its culmination in
A gourmet's dinner and the pleasing sight
Of bubbles in a magnum of champagne!

VI. WORDS AND MUSIC

Having as a student suffered
Hours of concentrated effort
On intricacies of form and
Counterpoint and orchestration,
Agonies of trial and error,
Doubt, derision and despair,
I finally relinquished
My ambition to compose,
And wisely put aside the
Fruits of wasted labour on
What was, alas, not genius
But a minor talent.

If musical creation were
To be denied me, verbal
Virtuosity was not, for from
My childhood I had felt
A close affinity with words,
And real fulfilment in their
Colour and significance.
The prose of every day I found
Too practical and too precise.
It lacked the rhythmic impetus,
The lilt and grace and movement
That I, as a musician, felt
Instinctively would give
Melodic shape to sentences,
A verbal cantilena like
The phrasing of a song.

I had often found myself
In company with young composers
Eager to experiment
With newer forms of musical
Expression, offering me all sorts
Of vocal works to try,
And finally commissioning
Libretti or new poems from
My miscellaneous collection.
Some of these would never see
The light of day, but served a useful
And constructive purpose, not alone
For the composer, for I also
Learnt a lesson – in humility.

I usually gave the first performance
Of these songs, but did not always
Find them easy to interpret.
There is a strange ambivalence
About a poem, whose initial
Concept had been mine, when newly
Clothed in vestments of another's vision.
This has always given me
A sense of shock, for it is never
What I have expected, though
At times – and I do not deny it –
It is much enhanced by music,
Given emphasis and life,
But often facing quite
Another way, projected in
A different direction.
Librettists have to be prepared
To have their texts subjected to
Whatever alterations the
Composer may think necessary
To the structure of his music.

It was wiser, therefore,
To withdraw from my involvement
In the poetry,
And leave Procrustes free to
Amputate, foreshorten or
Curtail it as he wished.

I have been fortunate, however,
For not all composers are
So arbitrary: most achieve
Impressive unity with my
Intention, and although the music
Naturally takes precedence
Above the text, it does not do so
At the poetry's expense.
But oh! how much I envy those
Particularly gifted minds
Who have the means to build,
From empty sheets of music manuscript,
Great masterpieces that delight
And overwhelm and elevate
The listening spirit!
Words no doubt are very fine,
But music has a special shrine!

VII. RECITAL

(i)

The soloist's recital is perhaps
The most demanding of all forms of musical
Expression – the ultimate in challenge and
Achievement for all singers. To present
A programme of so many different types
Of songs – an average of twenty-three
Or four – requiring total changes of
Emotion, mood and style and atmosphere
Within the space of several minutes, needs
A high degree of mental stamina,
Endurance, concentration, versatility
And accurate, unfailing memory.

Writer, painter and composer leave
Their masterpieces permanently on
The page or canvas or on music manuscript
For all the world's inspection at its leisure
And posterity to judge, unlike
Performing artists, who well know that *they*
Are judged upon the strength or weakness of
Their previous performance! They must work
In a perpetual state of creativity,
A constant struggle to maintain and to
Improve upon their own achievement, to be
Re-assessed at every future hearing.
A certain element of risk always
Attends a live performance, in the case
Of singers more than any other artist,
For they themselves are their own instrument,
Subject to the hazards of their health

And their emotions, both of which must be
In tune for this, the most exacting but
Rewarding aspect of their whole profession.

(ii)

All preparations are complete, the early
Months well spent in endless burrowing
Among the network of one's repertoire –
For there is so much choice, even in
The confines of a chosen realm, which in
My case has always been the music from
The vocal wealth of France, from early centuries
To present day. This is not to say
That I have not found constant pleasure
In the works of other nationalities,
Particularly Bach and Mozart,
Handel and Purcell and Britten,
Schubert, Monteverdi and those early
Multi-national musicians, who
Would wander through the courts of Europe
Writing at request of high born patrons.
But I found a special fascination
In the music of the French composers,
Whose restraint and elegance of style
Is typical of all their work, and so
Took every opportunity to build
Recital programmes from that repertoire.

(iii)

Those last few minutes in the artists' room
Before the concert starts I count among
The worst times of my life. There can be now
No turning back, nowhere to hide from one's
Deficiencies, for these will be exposed

To merciless and thorough scrutiny
From critical, expectant connoisseurs
Beyond the platform boundary: and no
Escape from that familiar and crowning
Cowardice – that inner sense of failure,
Doubt and personal inadequacy
That most artists nurture in their tortured
Consciousness to some degree or other
At such times as these. The singer who
Steps blithely out on to the platform in
A state of self-assured serenity,
Without the smallest variation in his
Pulse, (if he exists!) cannot hope
To give a sensitive portrayal, or
Impress that small but knowledgeable minority
That guards its values jealously and is not
Wooed by brouhaha and ballyhoo.

Although I have lost count of all the times
I have been through this agonising mixture
Of exquisite terror and determination,
Custom never lessens the initial
Tension of the first few minutes on the stage.
In singing with ensemble or with orchestra,
Or with the trappings of the operatic scene
In full support, there is a world of difference
From the strain of singing on your own,
Unattended save by your accompanist –
(Your lifeline, incidentally, during
The coming marathon! Where would you be
Without the solid comfort of his presence,
Calm and imperturbable and ready,
At the very second of emergency,
To save the situation by his speed
And cunning and dexterity?) But now,
You stand alone, and there is nothing left

[121]

To do but put anxiety into
The willing hands of God – and sing.

(iv)

The delicacy and precision of
My first short aria by Campra soon
Dispels all former terrors, since it needs
All our attention to negotiate
Successfully its fleeting runs and roulades.
The audience responds and we establish
An encouraging rapport, and imperceptibly
Move on beyond the studied confines of
The printed page. Though hours of meticulous
Rehearsal may have laid the basic framework
Of intention, always in the end
There is a subtle difference in result,
For each performance yields to inspiration
Of the moment. Though I have sung a song
A hundred times, there are as many variants
Of its interpretation, emanating
From that strange, mysterious alloy
Of poetry and music. Soon,
Both singer and accompanist will reach
That stage of effortless communication
That arises from a total harmony
Of thought which in its turn will then invite
The warm involvement of their audience
To share in these high moments of delight. . . .

And then next morning comes the true finale
That translates the warmth of live performance
Into judgements on a printed page.
Yet we are prey to other criticism;
None of us deceive ourselves,
And whether critics carp or praise
By spoken thought or written word,

The artists know when in their ease
And pleasure in performance they
Have found the very highest source
Of their fulfilment and reward.